INVENTIONS

James Nixon

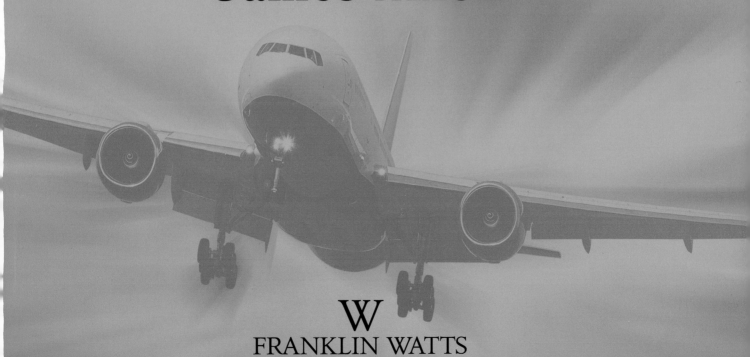

W

FRANKLIN WATTS

LONDON • SYDNEY

First published in 2013
by Franklin Watts

Copyright © Franklin Watts 2013

Franklin Watts
338 Euston Road
London NW1 3BH

Franklin Watts Australia
Level 17/207 Kent Street
Sydney, NSW 2000

Series Editor: Amy Stephenson
Planning and production by Discovery Books Ltd
Editor: James Nixon
Series Designer: D.R. ink
Picture researcher: James Nixon
Picture credits: cover image (Popular Science/Getty Images)
Alamy: pp. 12 (INTERFOTO), 20 (Mary Evans Picture Library). Corbis: pp. 9 bottom (PoodlesRock), 16 (Jerry Cooke), 27 bottom (Karen Kasmauski). Mary Evans Picture Library: pp. 5 top-left (INTERFOTO/Sammlung Rauch), 6 bottom (Illustrated London News Ltd), 9 top (Everett Collection), 10 top. Getty Images: pp. 11 top (Popperfoto), 13 bottom (Time & Life Pictures), 14 bottom (Gamma-Keystone), 18 (SSPL), 22 top (Fox Photos/ Stringer), 29 bottom (John B Carnett/Popular Science). NASA: pp. 22 bottom, 23 bottom. Shutterstock: pp. 4 top (cromic), 4 bottom-left (martan), 7 bottom (Fernando Cortes), 11 bottom (Kim Reinick), 14 top (Maxx-Studio), 15 bottom (Slobodan Djajic), 17 top (MADDRAT), 17 bottom (Odua Images), 19 top (Nikonaft), 19 bottom (MO_SES), 21 middle (ssguy), 24 top (Zerbor), 24 middle (ktsdesign), 25 bottom (Danilo Ducak), 26 top (Dmitry Kalinovsky), 26 bottom (Philip Lange), 27 top (Africa Studio), 27 middle (Sally Scott), 28 top (Shvaygert Ekaterina), 28 bottom-left (koya979), 28 bottom-right (Valerie Potapova), 29 top (Apples Eyes Studio). Wikimedia: pp. 4 bottom-right, 5 top-right, 5 bottom (Unbiassed), 6 top, 7 top (Vassil), 8 (Luigi Chiesa), 10 bottom (Andreas Praefcke), 13 top (Redrum0486), 15 top (Library of Congress), 15 middle (Norman Bruderhofer), 21 top, 21 bottom (Library of Congress), 23 top, 24 bottom, 25 top (Staff Sgt Aaron Allmon II).

Dewey number 600
ISBN: 978 1 4451 1828 4
Library ebook ISBN: 978 1 4451 2543 5

Printed in China

Franklin Watts is a division of Hachette Children's Books,
an Hachette UK company.
www.hachette.co.uk

CONTENTS

All words in **bold** can be found in the glossary on page 31.

THE ART OF INVENTION

Without inventors and inventions you wouldn't be able to talk to your friends on your mobile phone, play computer games, listen to music or even read this book. In fact you might still be living in a cave! Throughout history, people have invented things to make their lives better.

INVENTIONS JOKE

Q What did the useless inventor invent?

A A black highlighter pen, a waterproof sponge and an inflatable dartboard!

CHANGING INVENTIONS

The earliest inventions were simple tools, such as axes, hammers, knives and needles. Over time inventions change, as inventors improve on their designs. Someone had the bright idea to add a handle to an axe thousands of years after the first stone ones were made. The wheel appeared around 5,000 years ago. The first ones were solid pieces of tree trunk. Now wheels have tyres and spokes and are made out of metal.

Spoke

This picture shows a horse-drawn carriage from 2500BCE. The carriage has solid wooden discs for wheels.

One of the most successful inventions ever was German inventor Johannes Gutenberg's printing press, made in the 1450s. His device had a wooden frame that held a flat board with paper on top. This was pressed down onto another flat board that held words covered with ink. Using this machine, 150 million books were published across Europe by the end of the 1500s.

HOW DO INVENTIONS HAPPEN?

Some inventions are made very quickly by one person. Others take years of hard work, often by teams of people. An inventor can be the first person to think of an idea; the first person to make something; or the first person to make a device work really well so that people want to buy it.

Inventions can make inventors rich and famous. To stop people stealing their ideas and making money from them, inventors have to gain a **patent**. In today's smartphones there are an incredible 250,000 patented pieces of technology.

The United States of America

The Commissioner of Patents and Trademarks

Has received an application for a patent for a new and useful invention. The title and description of the invention are enclosed. The requirements of law have been complied with, and it has been determined that a patent on the invention shall be granted under the law.

Therefore, this   5,860,492

United States Patent

Grants to the person(s) having title to this patent the right to exclude others from making, using, offering for sale, or selling the invention throughout the United States of America or importing the invention into the United States of America for the term set forth below, subject to the payment of maintenance fees as provided by law.

If this application was filed prior to June 8, 1995, the term of this patent is the longer of seventeen years from the date of grant of this patent or twenty years from the earliest effective U.S. filing date of the application, subject to any statutory extension.

If this application was filed on or after June 8, 1995, the term of this patent is twenty years from the U.S. filing date, subject to any statutory extension. If the application contains a specific reference to an earlier filed application or applications under 35 U.S.C. 120, 121 or 365(c), the term of the patent is twenty years from the date on which the earliest application was filed, subject to any statutory extension.

Acting Commissioner of Patents and Trademarks

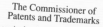

Inventors are given a certificate like this when they are awarded a patent for an invention.

TRUE OR FALSE?

There have been 400 patents issued for different designs of mousetrap. **True or False?**

FALSE! Over 4,400 designs of mousetrap have been patented. However, only about 20 of these made their inventors any money!

MATERIALS

Not all inventions are devices – some are brand new materials. Inventors can then use these materials to create new inventions.

ANCIENT INVENTIONS

Glass-blowing was invented in Syria in the first century CE. Craftsmen could pick up a blob of melted glass on the end of an iron tube and then blow it to shape glass vases, bowls and bottles. Glass-blowers still make glass in the same way today.

Ts'ai Lun from China invented the kind of paper we use today in 105CE. By crushing old rags and the bark of mulberry trees he made a porridge-like **pulp**. This was then flattened and dried to make a sheet of paper.

Glass-workers blow air into melted glass to form a bubble which can be worked into shape.

TRUE OR FALSE?

One inventor tried to build a steamship that prevented seasickness. **True or False?**

TRUE! Sir Henry Bessemer became world-famous in the 1850s for inventing a way of making steel from iron. He became known as the 'great king of steel'. Bessemer suffered from seasickness and decided to invent a ship with a saloon (passenger lounge) that did not rock from side to side. However the ship was a complete disaster making passengers more sick than ever!

This picture shows a cross-section of Bessemer's ship built in 1874. The central part was designed to not rock from side to side and stop passengers from feeling sick.

MAN-MADE MATERIALS

- The first man-made plastic was developed by American John Hyatt in the 1860s. It was called celluloid and could be worked into shape while it was hot. When the material cooled it hardened. Hyatt used it to make snooker balls, ping pong balls and spectacle frames.
- The first fully **synthetic** plastic, named Bakelite, was patented by Belgian Dr Leo Baekeland in 1909. Bakelite is not affected by heat. This means it is safe to use as a cover for pieces of electrical equipment that get hot.
- In 1935 American Wallace Carothers invented a fibre called nylon. Two years later he commited suicide because he thought he had not achieved much. If only he'd known that in 1939 64 million pairs of nylon stockings would sell within a year!

In the early 1900s celluloid was used to make toys such as dolls. If the toy was left in the hot sun or near a fire it could melt.

AMAZING FACT
Stronger than steel

Carbon fibres are long chains of **carbon atoms** that are thinner than a human hair, but stronger than steel. They were first made by Englishman Bill Watt in 1964. The fibres are fixed into plastic to make tough but very light materials. It is used to make aeroplanes, racing cars and sports equipment such as tennis rackets.

American Stephanie Kwolek invented a synthetic fibre called Kevlar® in 1966 that is five times stronger than steel. It is used to make safety helmets and bulletproof vests (right).

ELECTRICITY

Have you ever felt your jumper crackle when you pull it off, or seen a giant spark of lightning? These are caused by the power of electricity. But who were the inventors that made electricity useful to us?

THE FIRST BATTERY

Big discoveries often happen by pure accident. In 1786 Italian Luigi Galvani was chopping up dead frogs when he noticed the frogs' legs twitched when he touched them with his metal instruments. Fellow Italian, Alessandro Volta, saw that by touching two different metals onto the frog's legs, a **circuit** forms in which an **electric current** flows. Based on this idea he made the first battery in 1799 (right) from plates of zinc and copper, separated by cloth soaked in salty water.

Alessandro Volta's first battery.

TRUE OR FALSE?

Alessandro Volta tested which two metals would work best for his battery by putting them side by side in his roast dinner. **True or False?**

FALSE! He tested the metals by feeling the sensation when they were put on his tongue. You get the same uncomfortable feeling if you get a piece of foil stuck between your tooth and a metal filling.

POWER TO THE HOME

City streets and houses were dark places at night until the 1800s, when inventors found a way of **generating** enough electricity to power thousands of homes. Frenchman Hippolyte Pixii made the first dynamo (generator) in 1832, which changed mechanical energy (movement) into electrical energy. It generated electricity by spinning a magnet underneath two coils of wire. One of the first power stations was developed in 1882 by American Thomas Edison in New York, USA. Edison's huge generators were powered by **steam engines** that spun the wire coils, inside a **magnetic field**.

By 1884 the large generators in Edison's power station were sending electricity to 508 customers and lighting up over 10,000 lamps.

LIGHTING THE WORLD

The **filament** bulb was developed in 1845 by an Englishman, William Staite. The filament glowed with heat when an electric current was passed through it, but the filament **reacted** with the air in the bulb and kept breaking. Thomas Edison and English chemist Joseph Swan worked on improving the bulb at the same time. Instead of arguing about who should receive the patent, Edison and Swan joined forces in 1883 and sold their bulbs under the trade name Ediswan!

AMAZING FACT
Finding the filament

The big problem for Edison and Swan was finding a filament for the lightbulb that did not catch on fire or break when it got hot. Edison (above) tested 6,000 materials from all over the world including coconut hair, fishing line and beard hair! He eventually found that Japanese bamboo worked best if it was baked first.

MARVELLOUS MACHINES

In 1873 a Belgian called Zenobe Gramme made the first motor which could turn electricity into movement. This sparked a household **revolution**. In just a few years electrical devices were invented that changed the way we cooked, washed and cleaned.

CARPET CLEANERS

The first electrical vacuum cleaner was patented by Englishman Herbert Booth in 1901. His cleaner used an electric pump to suck the dust up. Unfortunately the pump was so large it had to be mounted on a horse-drawn cart in the street (right).

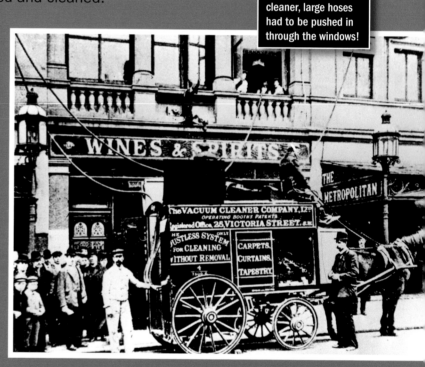

To use Herbert Booth's vacuum cleaner, large hoses had to be pushed in through the windows!

Mangle

In the 1920s washing machines heated the water automatically and a powered mangle was added to wring the clothes dry.

American James Spangler suffered from asthma and thought that keeping the dust down would help him. He invented a much smaller vacuum cleaner in 1907. It used an electric motor to **rotate** a brush at the front of the machine and a fan behind it to suck the dirt into a bag.

WASHING MACHINES

American Alva Fisher invented the first washing machine in 1907. It was little more than a wooden tub with an **agitator** powered by an electric motor bolted underneath. The water still had to be filled and emptied by hand and the clothes wrung dry.

It was the twin tubs of the 1950s that made washing machines really popular. Washing was done in one tub and spun at high speed in the other tub, which had small holes to let the water out and help dry the clothes.

GADGETS GALORE

- The first electric iron was invented in 1882 by American Henry Seely. It wasn't much use as it burned holes in the clothes! A year later he developed an improved safety iron.
- In an attempt to make their lives easier more than 30 women in the USA took out patents for dishwashers. The first machine was designed by Josephine Cochrane. She already had servants to wash the crockery but she wanted to invent something that didn't break her dishes!

AMAHING FACT
Microwaves

The microwaves that cook food very quickly were first used in **radar** systems. American engineer Percy Spencer was working close to some radar equipment when he noticed that a chocolate bar in his pocket had melted. Spencer tested to see if the microwaves would also cook eggs and popcorn. He then went on to patent the idea of a microwave oven (above) in 1945.

- Electric motors started to drive tools, too. German Wilhelm Fein had already invented the first electric fire alarm when he patented the first electric hand drill in 1895.
- The smell of burned toast was common when the first electric toasters appeared in 1893. All that changed when American Charles Strite invented the pop-up toaster in 1919.

COMMUNICATIONS

The invention of the **telegraph** and telephone changed the way we communicated with each other. For the first time messages could be sent around the world in an instant.

CODED MESSAGES

Charles Wheatstone and William Cooke patented their telegraph machine in 1837. A needle on the telegraph would point to different letters or numbers, depending on the amount of electric current that was sent along a wire. Samuel Morse's telegraph in 1840 sent coded messages along a wire in a different way. Using pulses of electricity the machine represented each letter and number as a pattern of dots and dashes, using a different pattern for each one.

TRUE OR FALSE?

The first telegraph sent messages using only ten letters of the alphabet. **True or False?**

FALSE! Wheatstone and Cooke's machine used 20 letters. This led to some odd spellings. 'Quick' for example was spelled 'kwick'.

FABULOUS PHONES

Following the success of the telegraph, inventors wanted to find a way of sending a person's voice over wires. In 1876 two men in the USA applied to patent their telephones on the very same day. Alexander Graham Bell beat poor Elisha Gray to the patent office by just a few hours!

In Bell's phone, a thin skin-like material shook when a person's voice was directed at it. The shaking moved an iron rod in front of a magnet to make an electric current. The current was carried along a wire to another phone where the same thing happened in reverse. The electric current made the iron rod move, which in turn shook a skin to reproduce the sound of the person's voice.

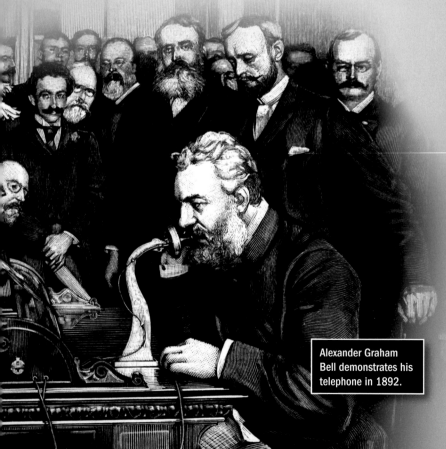

Alexander Graham Bell demonstrates his telephone in 1892.

AMAZING FACT
The first telephone message

Alexander Graham Bell was working on his invention when he spilled acid on his clothes. Bell picked up the telephone and called his assistant Thomas Watson, who was in a nearby room. 'Mr Watson, come here, I want you!' became the first-ever words heard on a telephone.

The Bell Telephone Company was formed in 1877. When the company built a network of masts nearly 100 years later in the 1970s, calls could be sent with wireless phones using **radio waves**. The first mobile phones (right) were not very mobile at all. The handsets and batteries were the length of a briefcase.

WORLDWIDE WIRELESS

It was Italian Guglielmo Marconi who saw that electrical signals could carry speech and music across the world using radio waves, without cables and wires. In 1895 Marconi developed radio equipment that could send a signal across a room in his parent's house. Gradually Marconi increased the distance. He could send signals over hills by fitting his **transmitter** and receiver with aerials, and connections to the ground called **earths**. By 1901 Marconi had sent a wireless message across the Atlantic Ocean from Cornwall in England to Newfoundland, which is now part of Canada.

PHONE JOKE

Caller: Operator! Operator! Call me an ambulance!

Operator: Okay. You're an ambulance!

Guglielmo Marconi (left) works on his radio with his assistant in 1903.

LIGHT AND SOUND

Beaming pictures from one side of the world to the other was much tougher for inventors than sending sound. Pictures are complicated – different parts have different colours. It was like inventing a telephone that could send a thousand voices at once. But Scottish inventor John Logie Baird showed the world that it was possible.

Baird began working on his television in 1923. His device scanned an image by using a spinning disc that had a spiral of holes. The light passing through each hole fell on **photocells** that changed the light into electricity. The electricity was fed into a **cathode ray tube** (CRT). When the beam of electricity hit the screen of the CRT the scanned picture appeared in black and white. Baird had little money – his first TV was built using bits of old bike, darning needles and a biscuit tin.

TRUE OR FALSE?

The liquid crystals used in television and smartphone flatscreens were first discovered in carrots in 1888. **True or False?**

TRUE! But it wasn't until the 1960s that scientists noticed that passing an electric current through a thin layer of liquid crystals created patterns. Liquid crystal displays (LCDs) started to replace CRTs in televisions in the 2000s.

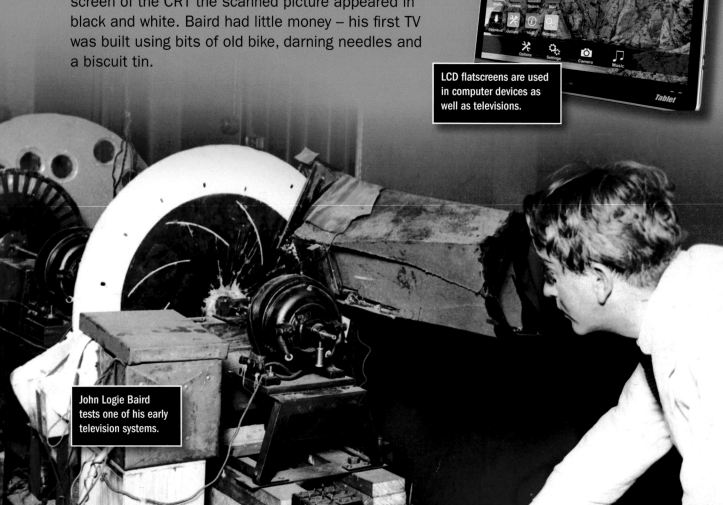

LCD flatscreens are used in computer devices as well as televisions.

John Logie Baird tests one of his early television systems.

MAKING MUSIC

The first type of record player was invented by Thomas Edison in 1877. His phonograph (left) was a work of genius. Sounds were recorded by a vibrating needle, which made scratches on a sheet of tinfoil wrapped around a rotating cylinder. When the tinfoil was rotated again, the scratches moved the needle about and its vibrations were turned back into sounds.

German Emile Berliner decided to use flat discs instead of cylinders in his **gramophone** of 1888. After a vibrating needle had recorded the sound, the pattern of scratches was **etched** into the metal disc with acid. The compact discs (CDs) we use today were invented by the companies Philips and Sony in the early 1980s. Sound information is stored in millions of tiny pits on the CD's surface. The pattern of pits is **reflected** back by a laser beam to play the music.

A gramophone from the early 1900s.

AMAZING FACT

Early photographs

Today you can take a picture with your digital camera and upload it onto your computer in seconds. In 1822 the first ever photograph taken by Frenchman Joseph Niépce took eight hours to **expose**. American George Eastman made a major **breakthrough** in photography in 1885 when he made a film that could be rolled up inside a camera. You snapped your photo onto the film and when the film was full you took the camera to the developers to have the pictures printed. Eastman's first camera in 1888 was called a Kodak and everyone wanted one.

THE COMPUTER AGE

The first computers were massive machines that took up entire rooms! Then in 1947, scientists invented something very special and very small that would change people's lives forever.

COMPUTERS FOR WAR

The first **digital** computer was designed by a German mathematician, Konrad Zuse in 1938. His computers were used to calculate the flight of rockets in the Second World War (1939–1945). The development of computers sped up during the war. The British built a machine called *Colossus* that was able to break the secret codes used by their enemies. In 1945 the US built a computer called ENIAC that was used to develop the lethal **hydrogen bomb**.

TRUE OR FALSE?

The world's first computer was powered by a steam engine. **True or False?**

TRUE – sort of! In 1834 Charles Babbage designed a mechanical computer that used wheels and cogs. It was so enormous that it had to be powered by a steam engine and only part of it was ever built.

AMAZING FACT
Monster machines

Early computers in the 1940s contained thousands of large triode valves. These acted like switches to control the electric currents, and looked a bit like lightbulbs. The computers had kilometres of wiring, used massive amounts of power and got very hot. ENIAC was gigantic – it had over 18,000 valves and weighed as much as six elephants!

ENIAC was over two metres high and 30 metres long.

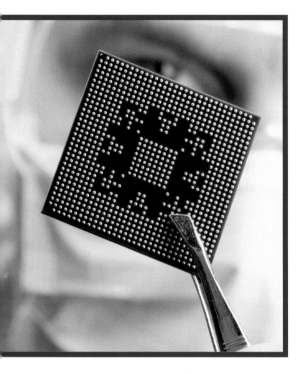

SMALLER AND SMALLER

The invention of the transistor by Americans John Bardeen, William Shockley and Walter Brattain in 1947 changed everything. The transistor did the same work as a triode valve, but it was much, much smaller. Today, transistors in computers are as wide as a single strand of hair!

The next big leap forward was the invention of the **microchip** in 1958 by American Jack Kilby. He spotted that if each tiny **component** was made from the same material, then they wouldn't need wires to join them together. Thousands of components could be crammed on to the same wafer-thin chip (left). By the 1970s computers were small enough to be used in the home.

THE INTERNET

The Internet was set up in 1969 so that the US military could share data. Computers could communicate with each other using telephone lines and radio waves because of the packet-switching system invented by Englishman Donald Davies and American Paul Baran. This system split digital data into small chunks, or 'packets', at one end and put the data back together at the other.

At first, the Internet was for scientists only. Then, in 1989, Englishman Tim Berners-Lee developed a system so that computers could click on links to see documents on computers around the world. By 1991 Berners-Lee had designed his first website and browser, and the World Wide Web was born.

A man browses the Internet on his laptop computer.

ENGINES AND POWER

Before the 1700s, the main sources of power were humans, water, wind and horses. Then in 1782, Scottish engineer James Watt started a revolution by inventing a new steam engine.

The first steam engines in the early 1700s created an up-and-down motion for pumping water out of the ground. It was while James Watt was mending an old steam engine that he decided he could do better. In 1782 he designed an engine that could change the up-and-down motion into a circular motion. His engines could be used to drive the machinery in factories.

AMAZING FACT
Hero's toy

A steam engine was actually invented in the first century by Hero of Alexandria in ancient Greece. In his device, two jets of steam were forced out of pipes to make a ball rotate. However, the Greeks thought it was just a toy and didn't do anything with it.

STEAM TRAVEL

It was only a matter of time before someone used Watt's steam engine design to create forward motion. In 1801 Englishman Richard Trevithick built a steam **locomotive** to pull carriages along rails. He called his train the 'Puffing Devil'. Seven years later, Trevithick took his idea to London where he built a circular track for his train and sold rides to passengers for one shilling (5p) a go. In 1825 George Stephenson and his son Robert engineered the locomotives and rails for the first-ever public railway. The trains carried goods and passengers on a 26-mile (40-km) journey between Stockton and Darlington in the north of England.

Large crowds watched the opening of the first ever public railway.

USING GAS AND OIL

The railways spread quickly, but steam engines were heavy so they were not practical for road vehicles. It was the invention of the **internal combustion engine** by German Nikolaus Otto in 1876 that made the motor car possible. The power in the engine came from burning gas inside cylinders, which forced **pistons** to move back and forth.

In the 1880s Germans Karl Benz and Gottlieb Daimler both made engines that used petrol as fuel instead of gas. Rudolf Diesel patented a new type of internal combustion engine in 1894, where diesel oil was **ignited** by highly **compressed** air.

In 1930 English engineer Frank Whittle invented a powerful jet engine that changed air travel. In the engine a spinning **turbine** sends out a jet of hot gases to drive an aeroplane forwards at great speed.

Internal combustion engine

Cylinder

Piston

Crankshaft

The pistons move up and down in an internal combustion engine. The power of the pistons turns the crankshaft. The power in the crankshaft is then used to turn the wheels of a motor vehicle.

AMAZING FACT
Engine blow-ups

The best inventors don't give up. In 1861, one of Nikolaus Otto's first internal combustion engines blew up and he was left almost penniless. Rudolf Diesel almost died in 1894 when one of his engines exploded in his face. Diesel had to remain in hospital for many months.

Jet engine

TRANSPORT

From around the 1850s onwards lots of new inventions changed the way we travelled. They included cars, motorcycles, bicycles, aeroplanes and new trains.

THE MOTOR CAR

The first car was a petrol engine stuck onto a horse-drawn carriage but it had no gears and couldn't climb hills. In 1891 two French engineers named René Panhard and Emile Lavassor built the first 'modern' car. It had an engine under a bonnet, a windscreen, rubber tyres and a gearbox. American inventor Henry Ford realised that the car would be a hit. He developed the first moving **assembly line** (right) in 1913 so that cars could be made quickly and cheaply.

In Ford's factories, the frame of a car moved along a line of workers. each of whom added a new part.

TRUE OR FALSE?

The first motorcycle was made almost entirely of wood. **True or False?**

TRUE! Gottlieb Daimler built a wooden bike and put a petrol engine on to it. It was first driven by his son in 1885.

BIKES

The first bicycle was made in 1839 by Scottish blacksmith Kirkpatrick Macmillan. The pedals were on either side of the front wheel and it was almost impossible to ride. The penny farthing, designed by James Starley and William Hillman in 1870 had a huge front wheel. It was hard to mount and even harder to ride without falling off! Everything changed in the cycling world when Harry Lawson from England connected a chain to the rear wheel in 1876. Bicycles started to become a safe and common form of transport.

Early bikes such as this one from 1868 had solid iron tyres and were called 'boneshakers'. The rider had to sit over a very large front wheel.

AMAZING FACT

The end of boneshakers

Early bicycles had solid iron or rubber tyres and were so uncomfortable to ride on the cobblestone streets that they were called 'boneshakers'. Scottish vet John Dunlop changed all that. In 1887 his son complained that his tricycle was too bumpy to ride, so Dunlop took the solid rubber tyres off and replaced them with pieces of garden hose filled with air. His idea of pneumatic (air-filled) tyres caught on and led to a much softer ride in cars and on bicycles.

TRAINS AND PLANES

Steam locomotives started to be replaced by electric ones in the 1950s. Inventors also started to design trains without wheels that could be lifted above the track and pushed forwards using powerful magnets! The system called magnetic levitation (maglev) was first used in 2003 on a railway in Shanghai, China.

Maglev trains can reach speeds of up to 270 mph (430 kph).

The first powered flight by an aircraft was made by Wilbur and Orville Wright's *Flyer* (below) in 1903. The propellers behind the wings were driven by an internal combustion engine. The first passenger airliner to use Frank Whittle's jet engine was the British de Havilland Comet in 1952. It had a top speed of 500 mph (800 kph).

INTO SPACE

The development of rockets in the 1900s changed the way we thought about the universe. Humans were now able to put **satellites** and shuttles into space and send astronauts to the Moon.

ROCKET MEN

American professor Robert Goddard realised that for a rocket to have enough **thrust** to get into space it would need a fast-burning, liquid fuel. In 1926 Goddard fired his first rocket. It only rose 56 metres into the air, but by 1937 he had fired a rocket three kilometres into the sky. German inventor Werner von Braun used Goddard's ideas to develop the deadly V2 missile (above right) for the Nazis in the Second World War.

Von Braun's V2 missile could carry an explosive **warhead** over a distance of 350 kilometres at a speed of 3,400 mph (5,500 kph)!

THE SPACE RACE

After the Second World War both Russia and the USA built rockets based on the V2 design as they raced each other to be first into space. The Russians were the first to succeed, in 1957. They put *Sputnik 1*, a hollow, steel ball, with a radio transmitter inside, into orbit above the Earth. Russian Yuri Gagarin became the first man in space in 1961 when his spacecraft *Vostok 1* orbited the Earth.

The next step was to invent a spacecraft that could return from space in one piece and be used again. The American's first reusable space shuttle blasted off in 1981 and the crafts continued to carry satellites and people into space for 30 years.

Rockets launch a reusable space shuttle into space.

LOOKING INTO SPACE

In 1608 Hans Lippershey, a Dutch spectacle-maker, discovered by accident that if he lined up two lenses he could make distant objects look closer. He used this idea to build the first telescope which he called a 'looker'. Italian mathematician Galileo heard of Lippershey's invention and within a year had made his own improved telescope. When he turned it towards the night sky he saw things that no one had ever seen before, such as the rings on Saturn and moons orbiting around Jupiter.

In 1990 NASA launched the Hubble Space Telescope (below right) into space – a giant telescope that uses mirrors. Hubble has beamed back thousands of images showing objects from deep inside the universe.

telescope to the Doge of Venice.

Hubble

ROCKET JOKE

Q Why was the rocket so angry?

A It got fired!

TRUE OR FALSE?

The images Hubble sends back to Earth are blurred because of a crack in one of its mirrors. **True or False?**

FALSE! Hubble did have a faulty mirror because it had been cut to the wrong shape, but astronauts were sent into space to fix the problem!

AT WAR

Inventions are not always made to benefit people – they are sometimes designed to destroy. **Gunpowder** was invented by the Chinese in the 900s. By the 1200s it could be packed into the end of tubes called cannon and exploded with enough force to fire missiles.

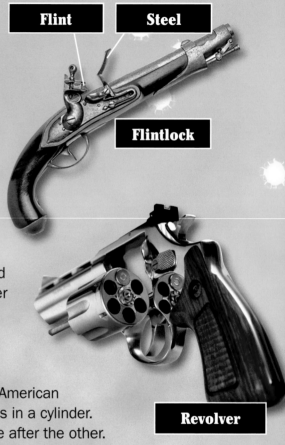

Flint

Steel

Flintlock

SHARP SHOOTERS

Early hand guns were slow to use because the person firing had to use one hand to aim the weapon and the other to ignite the gunpowder. The flintlock gun invented in France in 1610 was a good solution. When the trigger was pulled it caused a sharp piece of flint to scrape against a piece of steel. This caused a spark which ignited the gunpowder.

Until 1835 guns could only fire one shot at a time. Then American Samuel Colt invented a revolver, a pistol that holds bullets in a cylinder. The cylinder turned so that each bullet could be shot, one after the other.

Revolver

AMAZING FACT

The atomic bomb

In 1943 a team of international scientists led by American Robert Oppenheimer designed the atomic bomb, the most destructive weapon used in history. When the bomb explodes, huge amounts of **nuclear energy** are released. Two atomic bombs were dropped on Japan to end the Second World War. They destroyed the cities of Hiroshima and Nagasaki.

The atomic bombs dropped on Hiroshima and Nagasaki created huge mushroom-shaped clouds.

EXPLOSIVES

in 1846 an Italian chemist Ascanio Sobrero discovered a terrifyingly powerful liquid explosive called nitroglycerine. It exploded simply by shaking it. In 1867 Alfred Nobel from Sweden found a way of hardening nitroglycerine to make it safer to use. He called his product dynamite.

Englishman Robert Whitehead invented an underwater missile called a torpedo in 1866. The weapon was powered by compressed air and carried a warhead of explosives that could blast a ship up to 300 metres away.

STEALTH MACHINES

In 1982 the US Air Force built the F-117 *Nighthawk* (right), the world's first **stealth** fighter plane. The idea was to give the surface of the plane lots of different angles so it could not be easily spotted by radar.

Submarines are boats that can attack while they are hidden underwater. Irish-born American John Holland designed the first useful submarine in 1898. Under water it was powered by a battery. When it came to the surface, a petrol engine drove the sub forward and recharged the battery at the same time.

AMAZING FACT
The secret tank

During the First World War (1914–1918) the British invented the armoured tank for crossing mud and barbed wire barriers. Work on the tank was top secret, so it was called a water carrier, or 'tank', to hide its true purpose!

A lethal torpedo is launched from a submarine.

FARMING AND FOOD

People have been farming for at least 10,000 years, but inventions have dramatically changed the way land is farmed.

One of the greatest inventions in farming, the plough, was in use as early as 3500BCE. Ploughs were dragged along by people, and then oxen and horses. In 1933 Harry Ferguson from Northern Ireland invented a tractor that powered not only the wheels but a **shaft** that linked to machinery attached to the back. This let the driver pull and operate machinery such as a plough on his tractor.

TRUE OR FALSE?

The first **combine harvester** was drawn by horses. **True or False?**

TRUE! Hiram Moore and John Hascall invented the first combine harvester pulled by horses in the USA in 1836.

FARMING JOKE

Q Did you hear about the magic tractor?

A It turned into a field!

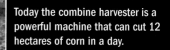

Today the combine harvester is a powerful machine that can cut 12 hectares of corn in a day.

A modern plough pulled by a tractor can plough four hectares of land in an hour. It would have taken eight oxen 30 days to do the same work!

PRESERVING FOOD

The idea of canning food was first developed by Frenchman Francois Appert in 1810 after Emperor Napoleon had offered a prize of 12,000 francs to anyone who could find a way of preserving food. Englishman Peter Durand took on the idea and patented the tin-plated can in the same year, 43 years before the can opener was invented!

In the 1860s Louis Pasteur from France was trying to find a way of stopping wine going sour. He found that **bacteria** made wine and other products such as milk go off. Pasteur heated milk to kill off the bacteria without affecting the taste. This was named pasteurised milk after him and milk is still treated in this way today.

FOOD FIRSTS

- American Clarence Birdseye saw that food would last longer if it was frozen. He realised that the secret was to freeze the food quickly so that it did not go soggy. It took him eight years to get this right, and his first packet of frozen peas went on sale in 1924.

- Crisps were first sold in 1920 by a grocer in England called Frank Smith, when he sliced up pieces of potato and cooked them in oil.

- A famous saying is: 'It's the best thing since sliced bread'. Sliced bread first went on sale in 1928 when an American inventor Otto Rohwedder invented a bread-slicing machine.

AMAZING FACT
Dolly the sheep

You might think *all* sheep look the same. In 1996 there were two that were identical. That's because scientists managed for the first time to **clone** an adult mammal. The cloned sheep was named Dolly. The successful birth of Dolly was after 276 failed attempts. Dolly was not made to be eaten – she was just an experiment.

Dolly the sheep was the world's first mammal to be cloned.

In the world of fashion, jeans are one of the most popular and successful inventions ever.

THE BEST OF THE REST

Almost everything around you has been invented by someone, somewhere. Here are a selection of some fascinating firsts.

· In 1873, American tailor Jacob Davis was asked to design a pair of trousers with pockets that wouldn't keep tearing. He used a material called denim and put metal rivets on the pocket corners to take the strain. This was the first ever pair of jeans.

· The zip was invented by American Whitcomb Judson in 1893 as a device for doing up boots. In truth it was pretty useless as it kept coming undone! The modern zip was patented by a Swede called Gideon Sundback in 1913.

. Laszlo Biro was a Hungarian writer and he was fed up with messy, inky fountain pens. So, in 1938 he invented the ballpoint pen. It contained a quick-drying ink that flowed over a rolling ball set in the tip of the pen.

- Microchips are not just used in computers. They are used in all sorts of gadgets from mobile phones to credit cards. Microchips were also ideal for bringing robots to life. The first robot was used in a factory in 1961 to lift hot pieces of metal and stack them. In 1966 American scientists developed the first mobile robot. They called it Shakey because it was so unsteady on its wheels!

- In 1816 French doctor René Laennec was struggling to hear the heartbeat of a rather chubby girl. To help him listen, he rolled a piece of paper into a tube and put it to her chest. He had just invented an early form of the stethoscope. Modern stethoscopes have rubber tubes, each fitted with an earpiece (right).

AMAZING FACT
Artificial body parts

Inventors have found amazing ways of replacing human body parts that have gone wrong. American doctor Robert Jarvik built the first successful artificial heart in 1970. It was put into a patient for the first time in 1982 and he survived for an incredible 112 days. In the 1500s French army doctor Ambroise Paré invented artificial legs and arms that could bend at the knee and elbow. Today some artificial limbs are **bionic**, which means they can be controlled by the body's muscles just like real limbs.

Bionic arms are incredible inventions. The wearer can use an arm to do normal tasks, such as shake someone's hand, unlock a door and peel a banana without squashing it.

QUIZ

How much have you learned from reading this book? Here is a quiz to test your memory.

1. Why should inventors gain a patent?

2. In which decade was the first plastic made and who invented it?

3. Which material is stronger than steel and used to make bulletproof vests?

   a) carbon fibre

   b) Kevlar®

   c) Bakelite

4. How did a frog help Allesandro Volta invent the battery?

5. Who invented the first dishwasher?

   a) Josephine Cochrane

   b) Alva Fisher

   c) James Spangler

6. How far had Guglielmo Marconi sent a radio signal by 1901?

7. Where were the liquid crystals used in television screens first discovered?

8. What did early computers contain which made them so massive?

   a) microchips

   b) triode valves

   c) transistors

9. Where was the first ever public railway built?

10. Why were early bicycles hard to ride?

11. What did Galileo's telescope show that had never been seen before?

12. What is the most destructive weapon ever used?

13. Put the following in the order they were invented:

   a) jeans

   b) tinned food

   c) dynamite

   d) the telephone

   e) the ballpoint pen

14. What was the first mobile robot called?

15. Unscramble the letters to find the names of three inventors:

   a) NOTES SAID OHM

   b) BEANS CELERY DICER

   c) RIGID BANJO HOLE

GLOSSARY

agitator a device in a washing machine that stirs and shakes the clothes to wash them clean

assembly line a system in a factory where a product moves along a line to be gradually put together

bacteria tiny living things that are only visible under a microscope

bionic describes a body part that has electronic components

breakthrough a sudden and important development or success

carbon atom the smallest part of the material carbon, one of the most common substances found on Earth

cathode ray tube a tube with a screen through which a beam of electricity passes before producing an image

circuit a complete path through which an electric current can flow

clone a living thing that is an exact copy of another

combine harvester a machine that can cut grain, separate the seeds from the straw and clean the crop all at once

component a part of a machine

compressed squeezed into less space

digital describes a device in which data is stored as a series of digits

earth a connection between an electrical device and the ground

electric current a flow of electricity

etch cut words or patterns into a surface

expose make a photograph visible

filament the thin metal wire in a lightbulb

generate produce energy, such as electricity

gramophone an old-fashioned record player

gunpowder a powdery mixture used as an explosive in guns and fireworks

hydrogen bomb a nuclear bomb with even more destructive power than the atomic bomb

ignite cause to catch fire

internal combustion engine an engine in which a mixture of fuel and air is burned inside cylinders to move pistons

locomotive a railway vehicle which pulls trains

magnetic field the area surrounding a magnet

microchip a thin piece of material carrying many electrical circuits

nuclear energy describes the huge energy released from atoms that are fired into each other or fused together

patent an official document given to an inventor, which by law prevents their invention from being made and sold by anyone else

photocell a device that changes light into electrical energy

piston a tube-shaped part of an engine that moves up and down inside a cylinder under pressure from hot gases

pulp a soggy mass of material

radar a system for detecting distant objects and their positions

radio waves invisible rays that can be used to send and receive signals

react respond to something in a certain way

reflected thrown back from a surface

revolution a sudden and dramatic change in something

rotate spin around

satellite an object in space that orbits the Earth, other planets or stars

shaft a long rod which transmits power in a machine

stealth describes vehicles that move in a secretive way

steam engine an engine that uses the energy of hot steam to generate mechanical energy (movement)

synthetic describes a substance that is made by a chemical reaction and not natural

telegraph a device for sending signals from a distance along a wire

thrust the force that pushes a rocket forwards

transmitter a device used to send a radio wave carrying a message

turbine a machine in which a wheel is made to spin by a fast-moving flow of water, steam or gas

WANT TO KNOW MORE?

Here are some places where you can find out a lot more about inventions.

WEBSITES

www.nps.gov/edis/forkids/index.htm
Find out all about one of the greatest inventors – Thomas Edison.

www.enchantedlearning.com/inventors/indexw. shtml
An A to Z of inventors and inventions.

www.funkidslive.com/podcast-channels/sir-sidney-mcsprockets-inspiring-inventions/
Listen to the stories behind some famous inventions on this children's radio station.

www.usborne.com/quicklinks/eng/catalogue/ catalogue.aspx?cat=I&loc=uk&area=S&subcat= ST&id=2377&topic=5277
This page has links to inventions games and quizzes.

BOOKS

Invention (Eyewitness), (Dorling Kindersley 2013)

Inventions (Weird True Facts), Moira Butterfield, (Franklin Watts 2012)

Inventions that Changed the World (Top Tens), Chris Oxlade, (Franklin Watts 2011)

Nature Got There First: Inventions Inspired by Nature, Phil Gates, (Kingfisher 2010)

Tales of Invention series, (Raintree 2011)

INDEX